JANUARY

Jemma Hathaway

January

Independently published

All rights reserved
© 2021 Jemma Hathaway

The right of Jemma Hathaway
to be identified as author of this work
has been asserted in accordance with section 77
of the Copyright, Designs and Patents Act 1988.

This book is in copyright.
No part of this publication may be reproduced
or transmitted in any form without permission.

Cover art by Simon Lowe

ISBN: 9798706504465

'*January* is a distillation of our shared, but very separate cultural, political and personal experiences during lockdown. Hathaway touches upon Capitol Hill riots, news briefings, Zoom calls, Amanda Gorman and *RuPaul's Drag Race*. With a mixture of modern life and the tiny miracles of universal truths, Hathaway's snapshots of January swing from political despair and relentless, ruthless hope to impress upon the reader an urgent celebration of survival.'
Kathryn O'Driscoll

'You know when someone manages to articulate how you're feeling better than you can yourself? Jemma Hathaway does that for me. Jemma makes you feel heard even though she's the one speaking. Her ability to be relatable in under a sentence, whilst creating fierce imagery that makes every poem on every page four dimensional, is breath-taking. Quick wit weaves mischievously between lines and inflicts a light heart onto heavy circumstances.
This collection allows hope to run free during a time when it is hard to hold on to. Her poems are not just for poets, or poetry lovers, but for anyone who is experiencing life in all its unpredictability. Jemma's words believe in their reader and give us time to believe in ourselves, and we all need to be believed in.'
Jemima Hughes

'I entered this collection tired and heavy and left with a smile and the desire to clean the shower. Jemma has a way with hope. Hope that is funny, as much as it is political. Hope that is honest and surreal. Hope that is offered through a depth of language. Packed with the ordinary wonder of every day, Jemma's movement between the moments and intricacies that fill our lives, are so beautifully observed. *January* is a collection for anyone who needs a powerful voice and a big arm around their shoulder - promising them of change.'
Rebecca Tantony

To Mum,
thanks for giving me life. I love it.
You always know just what to get me.

CONTENTS

AUTHOR'S NOTE

01/01/2021	ESSENTIAL TRAVEL	11
02/01/2021	WHAT OLD KNIVES REMINDED ME ABOUT THE NEW NORMAL	12
03/01/2021	TOO LOUD: A COUNTER-ARGUMENT	13
04/01/2021	CAREER CHANGE	15
05/01/2021	AFTER ANOTHER ANNOUNCEMENT	16
06/01/2021	REASONS TO BE CHEERFUL	17
07/01/2021	COMEDY IS TRAGEDY PLUS TIME SO MAYBE ONE DAY THIS JOKE WILL BE FUNNY	18
07/01/2021	TROUBLED WATERS POOL AROUND CAPITOL HILL	19
08/01/2021	YOU MATTER	20
09/01/2021	THE HURRICANE	22
10/01/2021	TO THE OTHER HALF OF US	24
11/01/2021	ON BEING GAY AND WATCHING TELEVISION	25
12/01/2021	CLOCK WORK	26
13/01/2021	TO MATT HAIG	27
14/01/2021	FORCES OF NATURE	28
15/01/2021	WHATSAPP GROUPS GET ON MY TITS	30
16/01/2021	THE ONE WHERE I USE A METAPHOR OF A GREEK DERIVATION	31
17/01/2021	TO YOU, READER. PART I	32
17/01/2021	TO YOU, READER. PART II	34
18/01/2021	WFH WTF	35
19/01/2021	MUM	37

20/01/2021	IF YOU COULD HAVE ANYTHING THIS YEAR, WHAT WOULD YOU WANT?	38
21/01/2021	TO AMANDA GORMAN	40
22/01/2021	RIGHT AS RAIN	41
23/01/2021	SEASON 13, EPISODE 4	42
24/01/2021	SNOWMEN after 'It's a Sin'	44
25/01/2021	CARBON	45
26/01/2021	THESE DAYS: A SHOPPING LIST	46
27/01/2021	DISCO	47
28/01/2021	ALGEBRA	48
29/01/2021	WEIRD	49
30/01/2021	TO THE OLD WAYS	50
31/01/2021	COUSIN	51
CHEERS M'DEARS		54
ABOUT THE AUTHOR		57

AUTHOR'S NOTE

Hi reader,

Yay! I'm so happy this book has found its way to you. Hopefully you will be too.
This collection began life as a project on Instagram, #NewYearNewPoemsSameMe and is full of poems written in the month of January 2021. I wrote a poem a day and there were two days where I wrote an extra one. I've included them all here. I hope you enjoy reading them as much as I enjoyed writing them.

Here are 33 things I thought in January…

Hope is a good thing, maybe the best of things

Andy Dufresne, 1966

*Do you want an adventure now,
or would you like to have your tea first?*

**Peter Pan, year unclear
(time works differently in Neverland)**

You better werk!

RuPaul, every day

What the fuck?

everyone, 2020

01/01/2021
ESSENTIAL TRAVEL

Your neighbour
is a train station,

you are accustomed
to arrivals and departures,

but when December boarded
and January alighted,

you'd never been so
mindful of the gap

between the train
and the platform.

On the concourse
the world waited,

nervous,
biting its fingernails

when January appeared, cleared
the barrier

with all that
baggage,

the world exhaled
and held up a placard,

it said only,
'Welcome.'

02/01/2021
WHAT OLD KNIVES REMINDED ME ABOUT THE NEW NORMAL

Today we disposed of five kitchen knives
that had lost their edge, covered them in
our favourite festive moments; every page
of the bumper TV guide, to be blunt

those are the only memories we made
this season, wrapped until they became
belated Christmas presents, we prayed
would never be opened, secured them in

empty plastic bottles, imagined sending
them out to sea as wounding messages
with dull points. We googled how to cut
the chance of damage from dangerous

objects once they are outside the home,
turns out we'd been doing it all year
and forgot, how shocking. The news
was on. And on. Telling us to stay

inside and save lives. Mask our faces
to protect only faceless possibilities
of people. It all came into sharp
focus then. We could never leave

those knives loose to make a bad
impression on a stranger, to seek
out the tender parts of people we
would never meet, make meat

of them. We are only gentle
in darkness, consider what
we cannot see, like it's ours
to keep safe. Isn't it odd

in this new normal,
old truths make
a very good
point.

03/01/2021
TOO LOUD: A COUNTER-ARGUMENT

Nobody cringes
at a canyon,

tells a mountain
it's too much,

asks a waterfall
to shut up.

At any moment over 2000
thunderstorms soundtrack the earth,

not one of them
shrinks to fit inside a library,

recasts their rumble
as a mime artist.

When you told me
to use my inside voice

it climbed back in its box.

Sometimes I am loud
because I have to talk

over anxiety and she is a bushfire;
rages, speaks in tongues.

The last time we had a storm
I stood on the balcony,

watched lightning expose

fault lines in the sky

and learnt that nothing
awesome is perfect.

Yes, sometimes I sound
like a thunderclap;

all I hear is applause.

04/01/2021
CAREER CHANGE

Loving yourself
is a full-time job;

for far too long
I had a zero-hour contract,

some weeks
I didn't make the rota,

some days called in sick,
went back to bed,

woke up in the graveyard
shift of life

and realised I hadn't
earned a single bonus,

so, I found
a hall of mirrors,

looked
and looked,

decided I was beautiful
from every angle.

Now when I open my eyes
I can't wait to get to work,

overtime is available
and I sign my name.

05/01/2021
AFTER ANOTHER ANNOUNCEMENT

We have become one
big casino;
lives are the stake,
the chips are down
and since time just turned 21,
someone's playing Blackjack.
Oh sure, let's twist again.
Like we did last summer.

Because I don't think we can stick
with this much longer.

We want to go out, of course
the mantra, stay in
the house, always wins.

But it gets hard to play
our cards right
when the game
keeps changing midway.

Have you ever been
to a casino during the day?
It's just an amusement arcade;

everyone at the tables
looks like they lost
much more than money.

06/01/2021
REASONS TO BE CHEERFUL

Flamingos exist.
They are out there in the world.
Peanut butter Marmite is an actual thing.
Sometimes Piers Morgan is asleep.
Smiles are free and spread faster
than any virus.
A hummingbird's heart beats
up to 1260 times per minute.
Now imagine that hummingbird
falls in love.
No matter what number is printed
on the label of your outfit,
you are the exact size and shape
of enough.
The world is full of drag queens
and so much wicked beauty.
Laughter is in your soul;
long before you walked and talked,
you laughed like it was the only reason to live.
There is no frown that can't be fixed
with a secret kitchen boogie.
Hope happens.
So does life.
And camembert.
You are here.
Someone, somewhere
is having the best moment of their life right now;

that person is me
because you are reading this.

Thank you.

07/01/2021
COMEDY IS TRAGEDY PLUS TIME SO MAYBE ONE DAY THIS JOKE WILL BE FUNNY

A mob of white supremacists,
one black activist
and an invisible clown
walk into a bar.
The supremacists rip
the place to pieces.
The activist protests.
The bartender shouts
'Get out, you're causing a riot.'

And escorts the activist
from the premises.

The invisible clown sighs,
because nobody can see how laughable it is.

07/01/2021
TROUBLED WATERS POOL AROUND CAPITOL HILL

The sea is a library,
it's bed a bookshelf,

with three million love stories
in the shape of ships,

still unread,
all with the same ending.

Some days the world is the sea
and some the shipwreck.

But today when the news
made waves

maybe you got capsized,
caught between the two

and it felt like the prelude
to an epitaph.

Well, your ending isn't written yet.

I promise the coastguard is coming.

08/01/2021
YOU MATTER

the universe is thinking about you

tastes your name under its tongue
slams shots of your spirit
considers a big bang
behind your back
just to turn your head

you do not

think yourself worthy
of attention

the universe knows better

sorts your thoughts
into a playlist

and listens every time
you sing yourself songs
about all the things you did wrong
yesterday

when two pieces of metal meet in space
they become one
and remain that way forever
have no way of knowing
they are not the same

it is called cold welding

the universe tries
to do this with you

knows to show
not tell
so speaks

in body language
because it is universal

nudges doorframes into your shoulder
skirting boards against your toes

lifts kerbs to trip you up
sends teacups
slipping from your fingers

finds all the ways
to throw
its voice and show
the green cross code
is not only for the road

Stop. Look. Listen.

remember how precious you are

how delicate

these are the push notifications
of the universe

do not turn them off

galaxies planets
nebulas space

all that matter

needs you to pay attention

and believe
you matter

09/01/2021
THE HURRICANE

Today I discovered a fanfiction website
for hypothetical hurricanes.

It states his name
was the first of 2020.

It was also the last.

The fandom has no clue
their creation Frankensteined
across the ocean on New Year's Eve
to do significant damage.

Maybe if we had paid attention
to the angle of his eyebrows,
the depth of his breath,
the weather reports,

we might have seen the clouds gather,

instead it tore a hole through the city of Sister,
ripped up multi-storeys
like love notes,
pulled lampposts from the ground like weeds.

When it careened through the house,
collecting a life
and stuffing it into bags,

it uprooted the trees
that help her breathe,

closed the year
by opening wounds.

If we collected the pieces of broken heart
scattered in its wake for miles
and made a mosaic

it would be

the photo on Christmas Eve
with all the smiles.

When these cyclones make landfall,
they weaken without the sea

and she is an ocean;
building breakwaters.

Hurricane vases are usually decorative,
they are not always the best home for flowers.

A hurricane does not look over its shoulder
when it leaves.

It gathers
and blows itself

to the next town clutching a structure
with a crack or a fault line.

Careful.

It's been nine days
and this hurricane already has a Tinder account.

10/01/2021
TO THE OTHER HALF OF US

On the days I am
tear 'n' share bread,
pulled in different directions,

you collect the breadcrumbs
and leave a trail of my name
to remind me who I am.

When my faith is stained
glass in the opening credits
of an earthquake,

you refuse to let me shake,
become shatter,
you remind me what matters,

when I am too lost
in space
to notice the universe.

You wear silly
like my favourite outfit,
no surprise you studied clowning,

you juggle my troubles
so easy,

thanks for never dropping me.

11/01/2021
ON BEING GAY AND WATCHING TELEVISION

'We NEED to watch this show.'
'What's it about?'
'Not sure.'
'Has it got decent reviews?'
'Not sure'
'Is it full of drama… suspense... intrigue…
anything interesting at all?'
'Not sure... but there are lesbians in it.'
'Ooh sounds good…
they won't be the main characters though.'
'Well, no.'
'And the storyline will probably be over the top.'
'Well, yeah… but hey,
we only need to watch the first fifteen minutes.'
'Obviously!'
BOTH: 'They'll be killed off by the ad break.'

12/01/2021
CLOCK WORK

I want to make time; turn
up on a factory floor, clock in
and manufacture moments,
for the January days it is hard
to pour a poem out of an hourglass,
piece together bits of minutes
into shiny new hours, crank cogs
of months into sturdy years
that stand the test of time,
watch fresh decades whip past
on conveyer belts, centuries fall
off assembly lines like snowflakes,
ages trundle out the door on
forklift pallets, send forever away
to warehouses, still
in the wrapper.

I am getting older.

But in this way, time
will not make me redundant.

13/01/2021
TO MATT HAIG

Every time I read your work
you outdo social distancing;
reach into my mouth
and take the words right out of it.

You sculpt wonder,
make clay of language
and remind me why I fell in love
with pottery.

I want to say thank you
for sharing Nora,
she is one of the best friend's
I made last year.

There were moments
when I came close
to borrowing books
from the Midnight Library,

that time you wrote
of how to be an ocean
I decided to try
and let it all wash over me.

14/01/2021
FORCES OF NATURE

In 1665 during the bubonic plague pandemic,
Isaac Newton discovered gravity.

In 2021 maybe we've disproved it;
some moments in this pandemic
I feel myself floating away.

Newton made his discovery
being struck
by the force of nature;

I tell myself this is the way to stay
grounded.

South American fire ants
protect themselves from floods
by forming rafts of their own bodies.
When it seems they are all at sea,
this is how they stay afloat.

Flocks of birds
lead and follow at the same time,
know they will go nowhere
unless they work together,
this is how they move forward.

The Siberian salamander
can remain frozen in ice for years
then thaw out
and carry on where it left off.
This is how it survives.

Change comes.
We won't be stuck inside forever.

Every day I remember to feel
the earth beneath my feet

and tell myself it is enough
to know the world is doing its work;

nature takes its course.

15/01/2021
WHATSAPP GROUPS GET ON MY TITS

Anxiety is the admin of a group chat
                                        you are always trying to leave,

most days you manage
                                        to mute the notifications.

You can't catch all the loose threads,
                          lose track of what's been said,

when your inner monologue
                                  is an unreliable narrator.

You try to make yourself heard
                                            above the din,

but self-talk is a raconteur,

                                even their throwaway comments
                                    go in the recycle bin,

return tomorrow
                                      as your clickbait.

Sometimes everything
is a laugh emoji
                              and you are still scrolling up
                                  to find the joke
but soon
                                      like, really soon
you will figure out your settings
                                  and press uninstall.

16/01/2021
THE ONE WHERE I USE A METAPHOR OF A GREEK DERIVATION

Nobody ever talks about little hills.
They're everywhere.
Half the humans on this planet have one in the garden.
Under a gazebo.
But not a south-facing aspect.
Because the world never shines a light
on this feature of the landscape,
so we keep it in the dark.

Yet so many people
spend time in the shade
at garden parties.

Clitoris is not a swear word.
It sounds a bit like clematis.

It's all just horticulture.

17/01/2021
TO YOU, READER. PART I

Maybe we've never met.
But you're reading this
so we probably get each other.

Maybe your smile
was a frown you found
at a second-hand shop
and upcycled
or maybe it was self-assembly
and it took a while to put together,
either way, it looks better
than the designer ones
you see on the sort of people
who would never pick up this book.

Maybe some of your best moments
were yesterdays
but you never let them
tread on your todays
and you still write letters to Santa
asking him to bring you tomorrow.

Maybe you wear a coat of mistakes
that falls out of fashion sometimes,
but you are trying
to care less about trend.
Maybe you buy self-doubt
right off the rack;
it's so easy to slip into.

Maybe you love travel
but perfection is a city
you never intend to visit
and your passport is stamped
with hell yes and fuck no.

Maybe your phone gallery
is a DeLorean

and when you hit 88
your eyelids become window ledges
and tears teeter on the brink.

Maybe you're still figuring out
what you want to be
when you grow up
but the only thing you're growing now
is grey hair.

Maybe you want to do that thing
but tell yourself you can't
because so many other people
are better at that thing
so the thing never gets done
and it's a shame because
you would slay at it
and nobody can do that thing
the way you would do it.

Maybe you think
there isn't enough time left.

Maybe
you need a new watch.

17/01/2021
TO YOU, READER. PART II

There may be maybes,

but there are also yesses,
you're covered in them.

Remember who you are.

You scuffed prayer
caffeinated spirit
Stevie Wonder song
in summertime
midnight kite
splash of light
Renaissance heart

not just a work of art,
you're nature's best Banksy.
Like if Mother Nature
saw you in the street
she'd stop to make a TikTok
to show the world
how shit-hot she is at her job.

You are a fierce messy yes
of a person.

Don't forget it.

18/01/2021
WFH WTF

The loneliest minute of the day is the one after a Zoom call; when you click Leave and wonder where the world went. But life rushes back in the room and reminds you it's not so bad. At least you don't have to wear a bra. Or brush your hair (because your camera is always off now) which is lucky because you haven't seen your hairbrush in days. But your toothbrush you've used twice already, although you can't be sure if the first time was actually yesterday. Your favourite mug hates you because you never let it hang out in the cupboard anymore with all the other mugs. The fridge is your fuck buddy and you can't stop getting inside it. Your utility company sends you love letters, so you turn on every electrical appliance you own to celebrate. Your onesies are in a turf war, your make-up bag has separation anxiety, your iron has an injunction against you. Lunch is strawberry jelly and a Maris Piper potato because that is all you have in the cupboard and you wonder if you've inadvertently stumbled on a Blumenthalesque gastronomic revelation and should begin a YouTube series on creative artisanal lockdown cuisine, but no, it tastes shit and you're just going mad. All your colleagues are podcasts, you've developed a close working relationship with an artificial houseplant, the clocks tell lies, there is only one day of the week and it is today, and it lasts for the rest of time. You stand outside your toilet hopping up and down in desperation so your bladder can remember the good old days. You complain to your mate Houseplant about the queue. You play Spot the Difference between morning and evening and lose every time because, damn it, they just look so similar. That box of After Eights from Christmas is still in the cellophane because you can't make it past 19:59 without falling asleep on the sofa. You wake up at 22:07 with a horizon for a neck, stumble to bed, wake up five hours later certain this is the perfect time to begin the day and wander about in the dark haunting your own house. Breakfast is toast and incredulity. You look in the mirror and yep, you still look suitably horrific. And then oh God, it's another meeting. You watch the clock at 08:59. That minute has forever inside it. Then for a half-hour voices are your wallpaper, are all around you, inflections grow arms, give you a little cuddle, until it's over and you realise the loneliest minute of the day is the one after a Zoom call; when you click Leave and wonder where the world went…

19/01/2021
MUM

My mother cannot be diluted into a glass
half-full or half-empty person.
But should the glass get smashed,
she would collect every shard
and glue a new vessel
with the capacity to sail an ocean
as well as hold one.
When I am lost at sea
she will find me
and bring me home.

But on the way back
we'll have to stop for a cappuccino.

20/01/2021
IF YOU COULD HAVE ANYTHING THIS YEAR, WHAT WOULD YOU WANT?

This year
I want to shine so bright
the sun needs shades to look down
in my direction
and Cassiopeia hires me as a life coach.

I want so many new experiences
my pockets overflow with difference,
then, when someone asks me
if I have any spare change
I can say yes and mean it.

I want adventure before tea
and my teabags filled with happy.

I want to store my nieces' laughter
in empty Marmite jars
and taste joy every time I take the lid off,
nobody will ever say they hate Marmite again.

In fact, hate won't even be a thing.

I want hate to go extinct.
In the distant future it will wash up
on the Jurassic coast,
a shell of its former self
and a kid with twinkles for eyes
will use it to decorate their sandcastle.

I want everyone I know
to swallow so much rainbow
Skittles ask them for advice.

I want you to smile so wide
your dentist wins a Nobel.

I want our hearts to grow so big

the stars use our pulse rates to navigate
their place in the heavens.

I want all these things tomorrow.

But if we are healthy and happy
and here today,

all my wishes just came true.

21/01/2021
TO AMANDA GORMAN

Somehow you took a spoon
reached through the screen,
across the sea
and stirred my soul.

Now I can't help but hope
your spoon
is the beginning of the end
for pitchforks.

I would say your words cut like a knife
but they weren't weaponry,
instead a wand
you waved and gave
the best black-girl-magic show I've seen,
though this was no illusion.

A friend told me today
their son saw you on TV
and wants to be just like you;
my ribcage
became a balloon,
it was true magic.

I imagine a thousand black girls
in living rooms
eyes bright
as their melanin
seeing themselves reflected in
the television screen,
it means
hope came dressed in a yellow coat.

I read one day you will run for president;
I might move to America
just to cast a vote.

22/01/2021
RIGHT AS RAIN

Into each life a little rain must fall.

On Earth it's water.

On Venus it's acid.

On Saturn it's diamonds.

If rain had its own TV show

it would be Location, Location, Location.

If Goldilocks were an alien,

this is the house she would pick.

Our rain is *just right.*

So, when raindrops keep falling on your head,

remember how lucky you are.

Geography has given you a gift.

At least you're not Venusian.

23/01/2021
SEASON 13, EPISODE 4

There is a scene in *Pretty Woman*
where Edward tells Vivian
that people who love opera will always love it
and people who don't, may learn to appreciate it,
but it will never become part of their soul.

That is the way I feel about a *Drag Race* lip sync.

Denali didn't take less than a hundred
percent pure love.

If you created a museum -
a *Ru*seum obviously -
this week's lip sync would be
the sell-out exhibit,

where a quetzal slays
a dragon.

The moment those arms became a clock
you knew whose time was up;

on the runway
there were 'Trains for Days'

so Denali tore up the timetable,

in two minutes
took us somewhere else,

where joy is the thing with feathers,
ostrich feathers, Mama!

where struts put peacocks
out of business

and duckwalks
look a cakewalk.

When that Queen shed her tailfeathers
and the room got shook
without one death drop,
it gave me life.

Maybe you don't get it.

Maybe you don't even know
what I'm talking about right now.

But if you do,

you know that diva just turned it out
and

It. Is. Everything.

24/01/2021
SNOWMEN
after 'It's a Sin'

I don't cry often
though my heart
has hairline fractures

last night
Russell T Davies
weighed heavy,
pressed on my chest
and my heart broke
a levee

this morning we woke
up to snow
but it melted by midday

so much beauty
gone too soon

I hope

elsewhere the clubs are still open

and somewhere

in Heaven
three-hundred thousand beautiful men
are dancing
with Donna Summer

and there is no winter.

25/01/2021
CARBON

Diamonds and pencil lead are chemically identical.
This is why it is impossible
to tell the difference
between words and jewels.
Look close enough and you might see it
in the structure.
The form in pencils is more stable;
so it seems safer to make a home inside
a metaphor than a mine.

But both can collapse in on you.

26/01/2021
THESE DAYS: A SHOPPING LIST

- ☐ Bag of carrots, large,
  consume when the days seem dark
- ☐ Extra strong mints;
  for the times you require surplus strength
- ☐ Pyjamas,
  various: bedtime, daywear and dress
- ☐ Alexa,
  to tell you what day it is
- ☐ *Ladies & Gentleman: The Best of George Michael,*
  so you can hear the words 'Let's go outside'
- ☐ Slide,
  for when your moods have spent too long on the swings
- ☐ VAR,
  to catch the moment the goalposts might move
- ☐ Wi-Fi,
  so you know you can still make a connection
- ☐ 2021 calendar,
  retain receipt, in the event it needs to be returned
- ☐ Toolkit,
  for the days you feel broken, but things won't fix themselves
- ☐ Stick, (or alternatively 1 x carrot from bag, as above,)
  monitor motivation levels and dispense to self accordingly
- ☐ Variety of tuts and/or needlessly exaggerated sighs,
  to be deployed in the outside queue when you get to the shop
- ☐ Laughter,
  buy in bulk.

- ☐ ~~Belief that you will get through this.~~
  just checked the cupboard and you already have it.

27/01/2021
DISCO

In 2009 scientists discovered the Milky Way
smells of rum and tastes of raspberries

if all this had an architect
they loved a cocktail

maybe it's just
one big night out

planets are mirror balls
the moon is a spotlight

constellations are white horses
at Studio 54

down here
life is a sticky dancefloor

I am freestyling

when the music stops
they'll have to drag me off

I will throw shapes
until they throw me out

of this venue
just to hit up another

light years
away

but I have no intention of going
gentle into that good nightclub

here you can dance with the stars
by sipping a daiquiri

28/01/2021
ALGEBRA

Some days it seems everyone else
knows the answer,
has solved the equation.

And I am still copying it down off the board.

But I remind myself
it's better to take time,

doodle in the margins,

make mistakes.

Make enough to run out of red ink.

I've learnt more from art
and wrong answers

than I ever have from algebra.

29/01/2021
WEIRD

There is a piece of art by #DFTE
that says,
'Happiness is being confidently weird'
and considering I've been nowhere for days,
I feel seen.
It cast a spell.

Because I'm starting to learn,

weird isn't a horcrux,
but the whole soul;

it's where the magic is.

30/01/2021
TO THE OLD WAYS

Hope you enjoyed hogging
the mic
because the red light
is on, your time is up,
voice is hoarse
and nobody
is listening to you anymore.

When Trump trotted
out the door,
corkscrew tail between his haunches,
it was every one of your sort
exiting stage left.

When a cork is popped
it is both a celebration
and an eviction.

This is you leaving.

When we're busy with bubbles,
nobody cares
what happens to the cork.
So, off you pop.

The future has the floor now,
and let me tell you,

the audience is already on its feet.

31/01/2021
COUSIN

Today you are 42.
Happy Birthday.

In the Hitchhikers Guide to the Galaxy
42 is the answer to life,
the universe and everything.

When I was born
you were nine months older.
Still are.
As kids, we roamed the stars;

we were the number 42 then.

You superhero, me sidekick.
Our capes were Parkas
and our Batmobile, a BMX.

We were always running,
couldn't wait to get to the future

and when the grown-ups said,
take the long way,
cross at the crossing,
we never did;

traffic can't stop superheroes.

I wish we could spin the earth
just like the first
Superman movie,

rewind time
like a video cassette
and go back

to the days I'd visit
and the latch would clack

on Nanny's front gate,

before the engine cut out
you'd already be there
beside the car
and I knew,

good times were coming.

Soon,
the good times will come again.

CHEERS M'DEARS

There are so many people I want to thank for helping January become more than just a page to tear off the calendar. A great big massive really-just-ridiculously-large thank you to:

Monica Crumback and Holly Ruskin for proof-reading this collection and providing sound and super-speedy editing advice.

Kathryn O'Driscoll, Jemima Hughes and Rebecca Tantony for giving such kind, thoughtful and timely reviews of *January*.

My fabulous friend, Simon Lowe, for taking pity on me and my intended clipart image and creating the wonderful cover. Sending snogs.

Nadine Richardson for being a total lifesaver and performing the necessary formatting wizardry it would have taken me until next January to do myself.

Karen McMillan for invaluable advice around self-publishing.

Darci Walker for gifting me the beautiful story that made it into 'To Amanda Gorman.'

On 8th January I invited Instagram followers to suggest what I should write about the next day and chose two that resonated the most. Thanks to Samantha Sao (@_lavendersilk_) for the prompt *What is your centre, how do you align?* which inspired 'To the other half of us' and special thanks and love to my sister and the prompt *Heartbreak* which became 'The Hurricane.'

I also want to thank everyone who has supported my poetry journey, my amazing friends and family, and especially my mum and dad for always encouraging my writing. And of course, extra giant thanks to the other half of us, Shakira, for being so supportive with this project. I love you more than biscuits.

Last but not least, thanks to you, reader, for giving this book your precious time and sticking with it to the end, you're a legend. Now go do that thing we talked about on the 17th.

ABOUT THE AUTHOR

Jemma Hathaway was born on a Friday, because even then she couldn't wait for the weekend. She loves poetry, disco, drag and Doritos. She has lived all over the place and had countless jobs - some brilliant, some ridiculous, but they all helped to pay for some lovely pens. She uses them to write about social issues, identity, hope, life, light, stuff and things.

Jemma has performed at various spoken word events around Bristol, UK, her poems have been featured on BBC Radio Bristol and she was a finalist in the Bristol Lyra Poetry Festival Slam 2020. She is assistant editor of Blood Moon Poetry (www.bloodmoonpoetry.com/), was runner up in the Oooh Beehive UK Online Slam Championship 2020 and is the current Hammer & Tongue slam champion for Bristol. You can find more of her work on Instagram @jemmahathaway.

This is her first poetry collection.

Printed in Great Britain
by Amazon